Contents

Chapter 1

'I can't hear any music. Are you sure Tessa's party is here, Jane? In a garage?' Mortimer asked. He looked around in the yard, but it was so dark he only saw the shapes of cars.

It was very quiet, almost spooky. 'Not in the garage, of course, but it must be somewhere around here,' Jane wasn't so sure anymore. 'Tess said Jason lived in the flat above the garage. Because he works here, his boss lets him have it for almost nothing.' Carefully they walked towards the light coming from a window above the garage. 'Wow, you can really party here, there are no neighbours around to complain about the noise!' she added.

Mortimer wasn't sure that it was a good idea to be here. Jason wouldn't be happy to see him. But he couldn't go back now. And he didn't even want to because he was in love. Not with sweet funny Jane, no, Mortimer was in love with her older sister Tessa. Jane knew that and tried to help him, that's why she had asked him to come to Tessa's birthday party with him. A year ago Tessa would have invited him anyway. Back then they had been best friends. But now Tessa was more careful. She didn't want Jason to be jealous. He was her boyfriend. He was three years older than her and they had been together for a year now.

Jane took his hand. 'Her hand is much smaller than Tessa's', he thought.

Tessa and Jane didn't even look like sisters. Jane was smaller than Tessa with dyed blond hair while Tessa had long dark hair and was even a bit taller than Mortimer. But not by much.

'Be careful not to trip on old car parts!' They continued walking across the yard towards the building.

'Yuck!' Jane suddenly cried out.

'What is it? Are you OK?'

'Nothing, I'm fine, but I must have just stepped on something soft – do you think there are rats here?'

'No, I don't think so. And anyway, they wouldn't sit and wait till you stepped on them.'

'Well, I'd rather step on a rat than run into that dog!' she said.

'Which dog?'

'That terrible Rottweiler!' she replied.

'Who is it?' they heard a voice shout. 'Jane, is that you?'

'Tessa, for heaven's sake, switch the light on out here!' Jane shouted back.

A moment later the yard was brightly lit and the door next to the garage opened. Tessa stood there, grinning and waving at them.

Chapter 2

'Where's Jason?' Mortimer asked Tessa. He and Jane were sitting on a big, black sofa. It looked expensive.

Mortimer had given her a present, but she had just put it on the coffee table and not opened it. 'What did you say?' Tessa went to the speakers and turned down the volume. 'Just testing the new loudspeakers!'

He knew it was stupid, but he had been hoping that Jason and Tessa had split up and that maybe Jason was in Alaska repairing sleds, eating frozen fish or whatever they eat there, and would never come back!

'Where's Jason?' He repeated his question. Tessa turned around, tossing back her long dark hair. Usually she wore it in a ponytail. 'She's so beautiful,' he thought.

'Getting more beer. He thought there wasn't enough.'

So Jason would be back. Of course. Because if they had split up, why would she be having her birthday party in his flat? Mortimer tried to smile. He looked around.

The room was huge. There were two sofas, a coffee table and a shelf with lots of old Mercedes stars. 'Probably stolen,' he thought. 'Nice room,' he said, but he didn't really like it, especially not the big poster of a blond woman in a tiny bikini sitting on a motorbike. 'What must Tessa think about that?' Mortimer thought.

Tessa stopped checking playlists on her iPod and sat beside him. 'You're early, you know,' she said to them and laughed. Jane rolled her eyes.

'Well, it's after nine, I thought …' Mortimer didn't finish the sentence. He had thought nine p.m. was late for a Sunday. But he could see he was wrong.

'No, no one will be here before ten or eleven.'

'Told you so!' Jane reminded him. 'You don't party at nine o'clock!'

'This isn't a birthday party for kids!' Tessa added. But when she saw the look on Mortimer's face she was sorry she had said that. Only Jason and his friends were older, but she was 16, like Mortimer and the rest of her friends. And she was happy that he had come. She really liked him, but they hadn't seen each other outside school for ages. Tessa was always afraid that Jason would get jealous when she was around other boys. Jason could get very angry. Tonight however, Jason couldn't say anything because Mortimer had come as Jane's date.

'I'm happy that you …' she started to speak, but Mortimer got up from the sofa and walked to the window. He was angry. Surely Tessa was only Jason's girlfriend because Jason was three years older and had a car and a job.

'Jane told me your parents don't like Jason,' Mortimer wanted to say, but he didn't. Even if they didn't like him, they let her go out with him. Not all parents were like his mother.

His mother wouldn't let him stay out longer than two a.m. And only on a Saturday. But today was Sunday and he had to be home at midnight. They heard someone running up the stairs.

'Jason!' Tessa ran to her boyfriend and kissed him. He was carrying two six-packs of beer and had his dark hair gelled back.

'There's more beer in the car,' Jason said and dropped on the sofa, kissing Jane on the cheek.

'I'll get it,' Tessa said.

'Let me help you,' Mortimer said, and went after her.

Chapter 3

'Could someone play some music – p u - l e a s e!!!' shouted the guy coming in. There was music of course, and it was loud, but it probably wasn't the kind of music he liked. He was wearing a tank top and had a big lion tattoo on his left arm. 'A tank top? In November?' Mortimer thought. So far, he hated all of Jason's friends.

Mortimer's grey hoodie had long sleeves and did not show his tattoo. It was a very small one anyway. But his mother had still been furious when she saw it because he hadn't asked her. He had told the guy in the tattoo studio he was 18. He had had to go to three studios till he found one that didn't ask to see his ID.

Mortimer felt lonely. He hadn't spoken to anyone all evening, except Jane and Tessa. There were lots of people there now. Most of them were Jason's friends, not Tessa's although it was her birthday. They were talking very loudly, laughing and drinking beer. Some girls were dancing, but there weren't many girls there anyway.

Jane was dancing, too. A girl and a boy were sitting next to him on the sofa. Both of them had lots of piercings and they were kissing, not even stopping to breathe. He guessed that Tessa and Jason were in the kitchen, kissing each other, too. Mortimer wanted something to drink, but he didn't want to go into the kitchen.

'Maybe I should talk to Lisa,' he thought. Until a year ago he had stuttered badly, but now he only did when he was very nervous. Lisa was sitting alone on the other sofa. She had been his classmate once, but she had had to repeat a year. She wasn't even his type, so there was no reason to be nervous.

Lisa was holding an empty glass and she looked lonely, too.

Maybe he should go over and bring her a coke. But that meant he had to go to the kitchen first.

'There you are!' Tessa was washing glasses. She smiled at him. Jason and Lion Tattoo were standing next to a big red fridge. They were laughing. 'Can I have a coke?' Mortimer asked.

'Do you want some rum in it?' Jason asked and winked at Lion Tattoo. 'Yes, why n-n-not,' Mortimer stuttered.

'Shit!' he thought. 'Shit' because he had stuttered and because he didn't want any alcohol. He had only tried vodka once when they were on a class trip last year. He had got so sick!

But what would they think of him if he said no?

Jason took a big, dirty glass from the table and filled it with rum. Then he carefully added a few drops of coke. 'What are you doing, Jason?' Tessa asked.

'Cheers!' Jason said and held out the glass to Mortimer.

'This isn't funny, Jason,' Tessa said angrily.

Mortimer looked at her, then looked at the glass. 'I won't d-d-drink from that glass, it's d-d-dirty!' He turned around and walked out of the kitchen.

Behind him he heard Jason and Lion Tattoo laughing. 'It's d-d-d-dirty!' Lion Tattoo screamed.

Mortimer hated Jason! He hated all of his friends!

He wanted to get away as quickly as possible, but he had to find his jacket first. There were so many jackets

here now and it was dark in the hallway. He couldn't find the stupid light switch!

'Hey Tess, smile, it was just a joke!' he heard Jason say. And then angrily: 'Why did you have to invite your ex-boyfriend anyway?'

'He has never been my boyfriend! He's just a good friend!'

That was true, but her answer hurt more than Jason's joke.

Mortimer grabbed his jacket and ran down the stairs into the cold November night.

Chapter 4

On his way home Mortimer took a shortcut across a field. 'In winter everything here just looks grey,' Mortimer thought, and for the hundredth time he wished that his parents weren't divorced and that he and his mother hadn't moved here.

Mortimer put his hands in his pockets, suddenly feeling very cold.

What was that? There was something in his left pocket. Mortimer pulled it out to look at it. It was difficult to see in the dark. It looked like a small plastic packet, and inside it were a lot of tiny mints or something. But when did he buy these? And why were they in a plastic packet?

He started running again and in a minute he was in town and went over to the Sword and Dagger to look at the packet again in the light of the pub sign. It couldn't be … No way!

They looked exactly like those ecstasy pills in the anti-drugs brochure they had given out at school. Except that the ones in the pictures had hearts on them, and these ones each had a little smiley.

Someone must have put them in his pocket. Was this another one of Jason's jokes? Mortimer's face was hot.

He took the jacket off to look at it in the light and suddenly realized that something else was wrong. The jacket was grey, and looked new. This wasn't his jacket! His own jacket was black and was worn away at the elbows and shoulders because it was his favourite and he wore it most days. He had taken someone else's jacket and someone else's drugs. Were they real ecstasy pills? How could he be sure?

There were so many pills, maybe more than 50. Could the grey jacket belong to a dealer? His heart was beating fast now as he began to panic. He looked around. The high street was empty and most of the windows were dark. Everyone seemed to be asleep. It was very quiet, only the sound of a motorbike far away.

'Think!' he told himself. But that was difficult because he was frightened.

No one had seen him take the jacket. No one would know he had found the packet of pills if he didn't keep the jacket.

He looked around again. On the corner there was the souvenir shop that had closed some weeks before. In front of it was a skip filled with building rubble. He went over to the skip and took a closer look. Lots of broken bricks, an old toilet and a rolled-up carpet. Mortimer put the packet back in the jacket pocket, looked over his shoulder one more time, and then threw the jacket into the skip. He carefully pulled the carpet over it. Then he turned around and ran home.

Chapter 5

On Monday morning Mortimer's memories of the night before were like a bad dream. He was almost sure that he had made a mistake and that he had thrown his own jacket and a packet of mints into that container. How stupid!

Mortimer and his classmates Paul and Tariq were in the schoolyard chatting about a new computer game, when he saw Tessa coming in through the gate.

'Mortimer, I've got something for you!' she shouted and held up a shopping bag. Paul winked at Mortimer. Saying: 'See you later!' he walked away.

'You missed the first two lessons!' Mortimer greeted Tessa. 'Oh no', he thought, 'why did I have to say that? I sound like a swot.'

'Only geography,' she answered and opened the big shopping bag. 'Isn't that your jacket? Didn't you notice you weren't wearing a jacket? Weren't you cold?' It was his. Mortimer took it. 'Thanks.'

But then he stopped to think and his face turned white. So it wasn't his jacket in the skip. But whose was it? And, more importantly: whose drugs?

'I thought it was yours,' Tessa said. 'You left so quickly. At first, Jason thought it was his.'

'It's Jason's?!' Mortimer cried, thinking of the jacket he had thrown away.

'No, it's not his, it's yours. You just said so yourself, didn't you?' She frowned. 'Jason's looks a lot like yours. But his is grey, and I recognized that this jacket here was yours. At first Jason thought someone had taken his jacket, someone who was at the party. But then he remembered he had left his jacket at the Sword and Dagger the night before. He'll get it today,' Tessa explained.

Then she saw the look on Mortimer's face. She could see that something wasn't right with him.

'Sorry, Mort, you must be angry at Jason and of course you don't care where he left his jacket, but he didn't mean to make you angry. I'm sure the rum was only a joke.'

Tessa told him again – as she had so many times before – that Jason was really a nice guy and that she was sure Jason would never have let him drink the rum and if Mortimer really knew him he would see that Jason was alright and ... but Mortimer wasn't listening.

The grey jacket in the container was Jason's. Mortimer was sure Jason had lied to Tessa. He hadn't left it at the pub. No, Jason had realized Mortimer had taken his jacket and the ecstasy pills.

'Jason takes drugs? Is he a drug dealer? Does Tessa know that? Did Jason tell her to give Mortimer this jacket so he could be sure Mortimer took his? Is she helping Jason?' A thousand thoughts flashed through his mind.

'Mortimer, say something. Are you angry with me?'

At that moment the school bell rang. 'No, I'm not,' he said. And it was even true. He wasn't angry, he was just so confused. Tessa turned to go. 'Aren't you coming to maths?' he asked.

'Too tired,' she laughed.

Mortimer didn't like maths and the teacher explained things that Mortimer already understood again and again. So Mortimer's thoughts went back to the night before. What should he do? He couldn't go to the police because he had thrown the jacket and the drugs away. And even if he got them back from the skip, of course Jason would say they weren't his. It would be his word against Jason's. But what was even worse: if Tessa really knew about the drugs, he couldn't tell anyone. He didn't want to get Tessa into trouble.

Chapter 6

Three days later Mortimer began to feel safer. He hadn't seen Jason and he hadn't heard anything from him. But he was worried about Tessa. She hadn't been to school since the day she had brought him his jacket.

Cycling home from school, he saw Jane and two of her friends looking at clothes in the window of the small Oxfam shop.

He crossed the road and got off his bike. 'Hi Jane, what's up? Why's Tessa not coming to school?' he asked her.

Jane told him Tessa had said she was sick and was staying in bed, but probably wasn't really ill. 'School gives my sister a headache, you know how she is. And since she started going out with Jason it's getting worse and worse,' she said.

Mortimer decided to go and see Tessa. He was afraid he might meet Jason there, but someone had to talk to her. If she missed any more lessons, she would have to repeat a year. And he had to ask her if she knew about the drugs and whether they were Jason's.

After five minutes on his bike it started to rain. Mortimer decided to cycle through the old playground near the pond. That was the shortest way to get to London Road where Tessa lived.

Since Monday he hadn't gone near the pond because he knew that sometimes Jason and his friends met there. But surely Jason was working at the garage right now. He wouldn't be there in the afternoon.

Chapter 7

Tessa was lying on her bed watching TV. She wasn't ill. She didn't even have a headache. She had had an argument with Jason. Again. They seemed to argue every day now. On the phone mostly. About a lot of stupid things. But mostly about his job. She wanted him to get a real job or do an apprenticeship, not just help in a garage for a few hours every week. And he said that she got on his nerves and that he didn't want to see her.

'It's stupid to stay at home because of that. I should go to school,' she thought. Since she had started going out with Jason she had already missed school too often and she didn't want to repeat a year.

But what if he left her? She couldn't even imagine how she would feel. He made her unhappy, but she still loved him. Jane said that she was stupid. But Jane was too young to understand. Jane didn't love anyone like she loved Jason.

Tessa loved cars. She would love to become a racing driver. And if she couldn't do that, she wanted to be a driving instructor. She loved everything about cars.

The smell of oil and gas ... she even loved that plastic smell inside new cars. Jason had let her drive his pick-up once. He had been sitting beside her, but it had felt as if she was driving it alone. Jason said she was a good driver. But he never let her drive his pick-up again.

Maybe she still loved Jason because he knew everything about cars and she just loved it when he had motor oil on his hands and face. And he looked like a man not like a boy.

Tessa's parents had promised her they would pay for her driving lessons and let her drive their car if she got better marks at school. She would get her provisional licence and start learning how to drive. She sighed. She would have to go to school tomorrow.

Chapter 8

It was still raining. Mortimer had almost crossed the playground when he suddenly saw them. And what was worse: they had seen him, too. Jason was with a big dog on a lead and the guy with the lion tattoo from the party, who was cleaning his fingernails with a pocket knife. Just like in a bad film when the bad guys are waiting for the good guy. They were standing beside the swing. Mortimer tried to cycle past them, but Jason stepped in his way and he had to break hard and jump off his bike.

'Look who's here,' Jason said to the other guy. 'The little thief … I think you have something that belongs to me. I waited for three days, but you didn't bring it back. That makes me really sad, you know. So, where's my jacket? I might catch a cold in this weather and we don't want that, do we?' The dog pulled at the lead to sniff at Mortimer's leg. Jason let it move closer to him.

'If my friend Jason gets a cold, I'll get you!' Lion Tattoo thought he had said something very funny. He laughed so hard he started to cough. The dog barked.

Mortimer was frightened. In general he was not afraid of dogs, but this one ... it looked dangerous. He was afraid to move. The dog might bite him.

He knew they probably wanted the ecstasy pills more than the jacket. His heart was beating quickly.

What could he do? Maybe he could get back on his bike or just run away. He knew he was quick. Probably quicker than Jason. Or he could fight him, Jason wasn't much taller. But he couldn't run quicker than the dog. Or fight the three of them. Lion Tattoo seemed even more dangerous than Jason.

He had to give him the drugs. Get them from that skip and just give them back.

'Listen, Jason,' he said. 'The drugs are in a safe place.'

'Drugs? What drugs?' Jason spat on the ground. 'Who's talking about drugs? We are talking about a jacket, my brand new jacket and of course, everything you may have found in its pockets!'

'Jason is very clever,' Mortimer thought. 'He won't even admit there were pills in the jacket pocket.' But now Mortimer was sure it was drugs.

'I'll meet you here tomorrow. Bring my jacket. And don't make me wait again!' Jason said angrily and then they let him go.

Chapter 9

Mortimer was so frightened that he completely forgot that he had been on his way to see Tessa. He got back on his bike and cycled to the high street as fast as he could. Suddenly he was afraid that the jacket would be gone.

When he came to the corner he saw that the pavement in front of the souvenir shop was empty. He was sure that was where the skip had been on Sunday night, but now it was gone. Maybe they had moved it to another place!

He cycled up and down high street three times, not able to trust his own eyes. The skip and the jacket were gone. He needed to talk to someone.

Chapter 10

'Hello?'

'Jane?'

'Mortimer, where are you?' Jane asked when Mortimer called her on her mobile later that day. She was lying on her bed watching TV, her cat Toby was sleeping on her feet.

'I'm at home,' he answered.

'What's up?'

'Nothing, but ... er ... Jane, I lost something ... and now I don't know what to do.'

'You lost something?' Jane wasn't really listening. She didn't like it when someone called while she was watching her favourite soap.

'No ... yes, I have and the person wants it back, but of course I can't give it back.'

'Then you must tell that someone you lost it. And that person will surely understand. There shouldn't be a problem ... Wait a moment! Mortimer, have you lost my camera? How could you! My parents will kill me!'

'No, no Jane. I haven't lost it. I'm not talking about your camera. Forget it. Bye, Jane.'

'I don't understand ...'

'Just forget it. Bye.'

Mortimer switched the TV on and watched a documentary about an animal home, trying hard not to think of what Jason's dog might do to him if Jason let it loose.

Chapter 11

'Mortimer! It's almost eight o'clock! You'll be late for school!' Mortimer's mother called from the kitchen. 'Get up!' But he wouldn't want to get up. 'I could say I'm ill,' he thought. That way he wouldn't have to go to school and meet Jason on the way.

'Mum, I think I've caught a cold. I feel terrible,' he shouted.

His mother came into his room.

'Let me feel your head. Mmm ... Your head doesn't feel hot. Do you have a test today?'

'Oh Mum! Why don't you believe me? I really have a sore throat!'

'Come on, get up.' She smiled. 'What about some nice orange juice?'

'Mum, I can't go to school, not today, I can't!'

She started to look worried.

'I have a problem, Mum,' he said.

'A problem? What is it?'

'I have ... lost something that wasn't mine. And now this person I ... borrowed it from will be angry.'

His mother sat down on his bed. 'Son, staying in bed won't help. You have to tell that person.'

'But he'll be very, very angry!'

'I could talk to him, if you like.'

'No!!' Mortimer almost shouted. 'I mean, no, you don't have to. I can do it myself.'

'Why don't you tell him you're going to save your pocket money? Tell him you'll buy him whatever it is you've lost.'

Mortimer almost had to laugh. He saw himself going to London and buying some ecstasy in a club – that kind of club which he would be too young to get into anyway.

But ... of course! He could offer Jason money!

'See,' his mother patted his head. 'Now you're smiling again. Time to get up! And I'll give you ten pounds extra,' she said and winked at him before she left the room.

Chapter 12

Tessa was back at school but Mortimer didn't want to talk to her. She was Jason's girlfriend and Mortimer didn't know how much she knew.

After school Mortimer didn't have to go all the way to the playground to meet Jason. When he got on his bike he saw that he was already waiting at the gate. Alone. No dog, no friend.

'Let's go,' Jason said. 'There are too many kids around.' Jason wanted to get away from the gate because he didn't want Tessa to see him with Mortimer.

They walked down the street. When no one was nearby Jason asked 'Do you have … my jacket?'

'No, I haven't.' Jason stopped and looked at him.

'You know what I want. Give it back or …'

'I can't give you back the pills. I threw them away.'

'You threw them away?!' Jason looked around and then he suddenly kicked Mortimer's bike very hard. Mortimer almost let go of it. 'So just get them back then,' Jason hissed.

'I can't, I mean, not now, maybe later. But I'll go to the police if you don't leave m-me alone.' There, he had said it. He was almost stuttering because he was so frightened.

'To the police?' Jason laughed. 'And what would you tell them? That you stole my jacket? You can't prove the drugs are mine.'

'But m-maybe they can. You can't frighten me,' Mortimer said.

'You like Tessa, don't you?' Jason suddenly asked. 'Because if you go to the police or tell anyone my little secret, I'll tell the police that Tessa takes drugs, and I know because she gets them from me!' he laughed.

'So that's why she often misses school, it's because she takes drugs,' Mortimer thought.

Now Mortimer had to think twice before going to the police! He couldn't tell them even if he wanted to. Tessa would be expelled from school. She would never speak to him again. So he said, 'I could give you money. I have 20 pounds I could give you now.'

'20 pounds?! You must be joking! Bring me 200 pounds tomorrow and I'll leave you alone.'

'But I don't have 200 pounds! And I can't get that much money from my mother!'

'What about your father? I heard he works in the computer business. He must make a lot of money. I'm sure he'll give you the 200 pounds if you ask him.'

Mortimer's heart was racing. 'I'm going to see my father next weekend. But I don't think he'll give me 200 pounds. He'll ask why I need it.'

'How you get the money is not my problem. Look Mortimer, I'm a nice guy. Sunday night, nine o'clock, you bring me 100 pounds. Let's say we'll meet at the graveyard, at the big gravestone near the chapel.' He laughed when he saw Mortimer's face. 'And you can give me another 100 pounds next week. But if you're not there, I ... we won't be so nice to you anymore!'

Chapter 13

In the evening Tessa was cycling to the garage to see Jason. She was a little hurt because she hadn't seen him all week and he had only phoned once.

Jason probably didn't come to see her because her parents didn't like him. Her father always asked him lots of questions, like why he only worked part-time at the garage and what he wanted to do with his life. She was lucky her father didn't know Jason had a criminal record. He had told her that because he trusted her! But it was all in the past now.

Her parents were so boring. Their lives were so boring. Working all the time. Jason was not like that.

When she had started going out with Jason they had sometimes gone to the sea in his car. She used to go to school in the mornings, but after one or two lessons she'd tell the teacher she had a headache and could she please go home? The whole time her parents had thought she was going to school and the teachers had thought she was staying at home. Clever! All her friends were so jealous!

Well, they weren't jealous anymore. These days, Jason never took her to the sea. They didn't do anything together. Jason had changed. One day he was nice to her, giving her things, telling her how beautiful she was and the next day he wanted to be alone, he had no time for her. And then they argued. She couldn't understand it.

When she arrived at the garage he wasn't there. A man who was working on a car told her he was in his flat. She took a small mirror from her bag and put on more mascara.

Jason liked that. It made her look older. She knocked on his door.

'Why didn't you come to see me?' She asked him when, after a lot of knocking, he opened the door. He had been sleeping. And he had a terrible headache.

'I should take it easy for a couple of weeks,' Jason thought. On ecstasy he could party for two days and that was fun, but then sometimes he needed to sleep for at least twelve hours.

Tessa could see he wasn't happy she had come. He seemed cross and tired, and he didn't even kiss her as she came through the door.

'Jason, what's the matter?' Tessa asked.

'I need a coffee,' he said and went to the kitchen. She followed him.

He was glad he had never told her about the drugs. She wouldn't understand and she'd tell him he had to change, he was sure of that. Lots of girls were like that when you were going out with them.

He looked around for a clean cup.

'Jason, talk to me!' She was angry now.

'Come on, Tess, I'm tired.' He took some milk from the fridge and smelled it. It didn't smell good, but he poured it into his mug anyway.

'You never come to see me anymore, and because of your stupid joke at the party Mortimer hardly speaks to me when I see him at school.' There were tears in her eyes now.

Jason took her in his arms. 'You even look beautiful when you cry,' he said. Girls loved to hear that.

'Do you still love me, Jason?' she asked.

'Of course I do,' he said.

'Then why don't we go to the sea together anymore?'

'We will. But not now. Go home now. I have to work.'

But Tessa didn't believe him. He would go back to bed and see his friends later. He would never be there for her when she needed him. She knew that now. She needed some time alone to think.

'Yes, I'd better go home now,' she said. And she thought of her driving licence and her marks at school and the money her parents would give her if she did well. 'I have homework to do,' she said, and she really meant it.

Chapter 14

After she had left, Jason took his cup of coffee to the living room and lay down on the sofa.

'Stupid girl!' he thought. When he had first met her she had been fun. Now she always wanted to talk about their future and about his job and she always wanted him to tell her he loved her. It wasn't fun anymore, it was hard work!

But splitting up wasn't a good idea at the moment. She might run to Mortimer and tell him. And then Mortimer might tell her he had found the ecstasy in his jacket.

Chapter 15

On Saturday morning Mortimer went to his father's house in Brighton. His father had a new wife and a son, his brother Sean. Mortimer stayed in Brighton every second weekend.

Usually Mortimer went to the beach first. He loved the beach. Even in November when it was cold and windy. But today he didn't. He could only think of the money he had to give Jason.

'MoMo!' Sean shouted happily when he opened the door.

'You're old enough now to call me Mortimer, Sean!' Mortimer said. Sean was four years old. He had his mother's curly hair and blue eyes.

'MoMo!' Sean shouted back and ran into the house.

Mortimer ran after him and caught him. 'NOOOOO!' Sean shouted. He loved it when Mortimer played with him.

'Hi Elaine! Is Dad home?' Mortimer asked her. She had come downstairs when she heard them laughing and shouting. Elaine was his father's new wife.

'He's in the garden. Don't ask me what he's doing there. You can't work in the garden in November. But you know your father.'

Mortimer liked Elaine. She never tried to be his mother and she never told him what to do.

Chapter 16

That weekend Mortimer spent a lot of time online, playing computer games and chatting with friends. But he didn't tell anyone what was going on in his life back home.

On Sunday afternoon Mortimer still hadn't asked his father about the money. He didn't know how, or what to tell him.

At first, Mortimer thought he could wait until the journey back home, when he would be alone with his dad in the car. But as the hours went by quickly, Mortimer got more and more nervous until he started to feel sick. He couldn't wait that long. He had to ask him now!

They were having their afternoon tea when Mortimer had an idea. 'Dad,' he said. 'I think my computer has a virus. Can you check it for me?'

'A virus? Are you sure?'

'No, I'm not sure!' he said loudly. 'That's why I'm asking you to check it!'

Elaine and his father looked at each other. They didn't understand why Mortimer was so angry.

'Of course, calm down, it's no problem,' his father said.

Ten minutes later they were sitting in Mortimer's room in front of his computer. But Mortimer wasn't watching what his father was doing.

'Dad, I know it's only November ... but could I have my Christmas money today?'

'Mmmmm ... I don't think there's a virus. Why do you think there is? Everything is working and ...'

'Dad! I asked you something!'

'Don't shout, Mort. What's the matter with you?'

'Nothing. Sorry. I just want my Christmas money now and not in December.'

'What do you need the money for? Is there a problem? You're not yourself this weekend.'

'If only I could tell him,' Mortimer thought. 'But then Tessa will be in trouble.' So he laughed. 'Of course there isn't a problem,' he said. 'I just want to buy some new games. You don't have to worry about me. I'm OK.'

'Look, Mort, if you need something you can always tell me or your mother. If you want new software, I'll get it for you even if it's expensive. But if you want more pocket money, I'll have to talk with your mother first.'

Chapter 17

When his father drove him back in the evening, Mortimer was quiet. Before they had left Brighton, his father had given him 20 pounds. But that wasn't enough.

They arrived at the farmhouse in London Road where Tessa lived. Her parents weren't farmers, but they liked to live in the country. Mortimer had asked his father to take him there.

He still didn't know what to do about Jason. But he had to talk to Tessa first.

'Phone your mother and tell her where you are so she knows you'll be late.'

'I will, Dad. Bye.'

Jason's car wasn't parked in front of the house. That was good. So he wasn't here. Tessa opened the door.

'Mortimer! I almost thought you weren't my friend anymore! Come in.'

Her sister and her parents weren't at home and they went upstairs to Tessa's room. Mortimer looked around. He hadn't been in this room since Tessa had become Jason's girlfriend. She still had all those posters with racing cars on the wall.

'Do you want a coke?' Tessa asked. Suddenly she remembered the party.

'Oh I'm sorry, Mort, I didn't mean to … I mean, I wasn't joking.'

'No thanks, Tessa, I'm not thirsty.'

'Don't stand there, sit down.'

They sat down on her bed. Although she was his friend, sitting next to her now when they were alone made him feel shy.

Mortimer saw a pair of skates in the corner. 'I didn't know you s-s-skated,' he said.

'I don't, I mean they're new. I haven't tried them yet.'

Mortimer couldn't look at her. He didn't know how to tell her about Jason. But he knew he had to.

'Tell her now,' he thought and then he quickly said 'I know Jason takes drugs. Do you take drugs, too?' Tessa jumped up.

'What?! How can you say that?' she shouted. Her eyes looked so angry he had to look away. 'Did you come here to say bad things about my boyfriend?' Then she started to cry. She knew it was true. Jason took drugs.

Mortimer got up and took her in his arms. Suddenly he wasn't shy anymore. He loved her, but she was also his best friend. He told her the whole story.

'He said I took drugs?' Tessa asked for the second time. 'And that's why you didn't tell anybody?'

Mortimer nodded. 'Well, that and … I guess I'm very frightened of his dog.'

'Frightened of Chuck? Yes, I can understand that. Chuck isn't a nice dog. But he's just a big puppy really and a bit stupid. You know what? I give him ground beef when Jason isn't there. He's crazy about it. Then he likes me.' Tessa laughed a little.

'I'm going to meet Jason at the graveyard at nine o'clock,' Mortimer told her.

'No, you can't do that! You don't have the 100 pounds. He'll get angry and hurt you!' she said.

'I have to go! What else can I do? If I don't go, he'll wait for me somewhere – tomorrow or the day after tomorrow. It will never stop.'

'If you must go, why don't you ask Paul to go with you? I'm sure he'll help you.' Paul was a classmate and a friend. 'Paul won't even ask questions. He just loves to fight,' she said.

'Don't you see Tessa, if I do that then Jason will bring more of his friends next time.'

'Then go to the police!'

'It's my word against his. The police won't arrest Jason just because I tell them that he had drugs before I threw them away.'

'I think they might believe you. Jason has a criminal record. Years ago he got caught smoking a joint in the school toilet. And later he beat up the boy who he thought had told a teacher. That was before you and I moved here. He told me about it.'

'But he didn't beat me up! He hasn't done anything yet. What could I tell the police?'

'What if I went to the graveyard with you? I could hide somewhere and listen. I could tell the police what I heard. Then they would have to believe us.'

'No! That's much too dangerous. The other guy might be there too and find you. And the dog? He would find you.'

'I'm not frightened of Chuck. I know what to do with him. Wait! I have an idea. Do you have your mobile with you?'

'Yes, I do. Oh, no! I forgot to phone my mum. She'll worry about why I'm not home yet.'

Mortimer took his mobile and quickly left a message for his mum. Tessa ran downstairs and came back into her room holding a packet.

'Alright.' Mortimer said to Tessa. 'What's your idea?'

'You go to the graveyard. You can take my bike. When you're there you can call me, but then you don't hang up. Just put your mobile back in your pocket and leave it on. I can put my mobile on loudspeakers, so I'll be able to hear everything. If it sounds like it's getting dangerous, I'll come and help you. Jason would never hurt me. And take this,' she held out the packet.

'But ...' Mortimer thought about it. What else could he do? It was almost quarter to nine. He had to hurry. He took Tessa's bike, the torch and the packet and cycled to the graveyard.

Chapter 18

There was a stone wall around the graveyard. The gate usually wasn't locked, but the wall wasn't so high.

Mortimer decided to climb over the wall rather than go through the gate. Jason might already be waiting for him at the gate. Mortimer needed a little time to make that call to Tessa first. The wall was wet because it had rained earlier, but it wasn't too difficult to climb. He could see the dark shape of the chapel. The graveyard smelled of wet trees and wood but also of something else: a smell you only found at graveyards.

Everything was quiet. Jason wasn't here yet.

He had told Mortimer to meet him at the big gravestone near the chapel. Mortimer's heart was beating fast when he took his mobile out of his pocket and dialled Tessa's number. She answered immediately, but they didn't talk. That was too dangerous. He put the mobile back in his pocket.

Then he switched on his torch and looked around. For some reason the gravestones frightened him. When you thought about it, every gravestone was for someone who had died. And one day he would also die. Mortimer realized how stupid it was to be here, waiting for Jason. Jason wouldn't want to kill him, but what about his crazy friend or his crazy dog?

Closer to the chapel, under a tree, there was a tall gravestone. That must be the one where Jason wanted to meet. Mortimer walked towards it. He read the inscription, 'In loving memory of Mary Elizabeth' – Mary Elizabeth had died in November 1820. She was only 16 when she died. 16. The same age as him now. Maybe that was another one of Jason's jokes.

'Well, well, well, I almost thought you wouldn't come.' Suddenly Jason was standing behind him with his dog Chuck next to him. His voice made Mortimer jump. 'I've been looking for you. I told you to meet me at the largest stone!'

'Yes, I know,' Mortimer said.

He tried not to sound frightened because he knew Tessa was listening.

'This is not the largest gravestone!' Jason spoke very slowly as if he was talking to someone who didn't understand English very well or was deaf and had to read his lips. 'Mortimer, you're so stupid it makes me sad. I don't know how you get through life. Can you find your way to school in the morning or do you have to ask people in the street? "Excuse m-m-me, can you tell me the way to m-m-my school?"' He spoke in a silly voice and pretended to be Mortimer.

Tessa was listening. She wanted to shout into her mobile to make him stop talking to Mortimer like that. Mortimer wasn't stupid. She was the stupid one! She had been stupid enough to love Jason.

'I have to do something,' she thought. That's when she heard her parents' car. She quickly ran downstairs with her mobile.

Chapter 19

'OK, give me the money and then let's get out of here. I don't like graveyards. They frighten us, don't they Chuck?' Jason laughed. He liked his own jokes.

Mortimer didn't have a plan. But he had to make Jason talk about the drugs. He wanted Tessa to hear it. That was important. Today she had believed him. But what if Jason talked to her later and told her it wasn't true and that Mortimer had been lying? Who would she believe then?

So he said 'I lied, Jason. I didn't throw your pills away. I still have them.'

'You still have them? That's even better. I have a business to think of, you know! I may have lost some customers already. You know what? I think you should give me the money and the drugs.'

There, Jason had said it. Now Mortimer only had to think of a way to get away.

'I won't,' Mortimer said. 'I can't, I mean not now. But I'll give you 40 pounds.'

Without a warning Jason hit him in the face. Mortimer stumbled and fell. 'Who do you think you are? Do you think you can play games with me, you stupid boy?' Chuck was next to him, sniffing his pocket.

Mortimer got up, took the packet from his pocket and quickly threw it as far as he could. The dog was after it in a flash. As hard as he could, he kicked Jason's left knee.

'Ahhh!' Jason dropped his torch and held his knee. Mortimer ran. He couldn't see much in the dark, but he knew where the gate was.

'Don't try to hide, we'll get you!' Jason shouted. Then, 'Chuck, come here! Chuck, come here now!'

But Chuck wasn't listening. He was busy tearing apart the packet.

Mortimer kept running. He could hear Jason behind him, stumbling and making a lot of noise because his leg hurt. Mortimer looked quickly back over his shoulder. Jason was only a few metres away. As Mortimer turned back around, he slipped on the wet ground and fell over.

He started to get up, but Jason was on him now. 'You're dead,' Jason shouted.

At that moment Mortimer heard a police car. Jason heard it too and looked around. He let go of Mortimer and got up. He knew he couldn't climb the wall because his leg hurt too much. So he started to limp towards the gate as fast as he could. But Jason wasn't fast enough. Tessa's father was already standing at the gate, blocking his way. Before Jason could decide whether to hit him or call Chuck again the police car arrived and two officers got out.

At the same time Tessa came cycling around the corner. She had run downstairs to her mum and dad and let them listen to what Jason was saying. Her father had called the police immediately. Tessa had started crying because she was afraid the police might arrive too late. So her father had driven to the graveyard to wait for the police and help Mortimer. But he didn't want Tessa to come. 'Too dangerous,' he had said. But she had to be there! She had jumped on Jane's bike and quickly cycled to the graveyard.

'It's him, he's the drug dealer!' Tessa shouted and pointed at Jason who was standing there, not knowing what to do when suddenly a happy Chuck came running towards them, carrying a half-eaten, tightly wrapped packet of beef in his mouth – the packet that Tessa had given Mortimer.

'That boy over there attacked me!' Jason cried. 'I was only walking my dog, I haven't done anything!'

'We heard everything Jason!' Tessa jumped from the bike. 'Mortimer called me and didn't hang up his mobile. Mum and Dad and I heard you talking about the drugs!'

'Bitch!' Jason shouted at her.

Chapter 20

The police took Jason to the police station. The other three followed them in Tessa's dad's car. On the way they phoned Mortimer's mother. When they arrived, Mortimer and Tessa told the police everything they knew.

'What will happen to Jason's dog?' Tessa suddenly remembered.

'Don't worry. He's been taken to the animal shelter.' the young officer said. 'I'm sure they'll find a new owner for him if Jason has to go to prison.'

When Mortimer's mother arrived at the police station she was shocked. 'Look at your face! You're going to get a black eye! Why didn't you tell me about Jason?'

'I don't know. I didn't have any proof.'

'But you didn't need proof! I believe you, I'm your mother!'

The older one of the two police officers shook his head and said 'You should have told your mum. Or come to us. What you did was very dangerous.'

'But would you have believed us?' Tessa asked.

'Of course we would. Maybe this sort of thing doesn't happen every day. But we're seeing kids getting into trouble because of drugs more and more often around here. Drugs don't only exist in big cities.' He smiled at them. 'But of course you know that now.'

'I guess I was pretty stupid,' Mortimer shrugged. 'It was my fault Jason was so angry. I mean, I did throw away his drugs, I owed him the money.'

'You're wrong,' the young officer said. 'Throwing away the drugs and not going to the police wasn't a good idea, but it's not a crime either. However, using and selling drugs and threatening people is a crime. And that's what Jason did. And now I think it's time for you to go home with your parents. We'll take care of Jason.'

'We really have to talk about it all again. But let's all go home now, we're all tired,' Tessa's father said when they were all standing outside the police station.

'Let me say good night to Mortimer first,' Tessa said. She went over to him. 'I made a mistake, Mortimer.'

'No, you didn't. You were right to tell your parents.'

'I don't mean that. I mean ... Jason. I thought he loved me and I ... but he didn't. Not really. I know that now. But you and I ... maybe we can ...'

'... go to the cinema tomorrow?' Mortimer asked and smiled at her.

'Yes,' she said and kissed him.

Vocabulary

Abbreviations

AE = American English
BE = British English
sb. = somebody
sth. = something
etw. = etwas
jdm. = jemandem
umg. = umgangssprachlich

A

(to) **admit** [əd'mɪt] zugeben
animal shelter ['ænɪml 'ʃeltə] Tierheim
apprenticeship [ə'prentɪʃip] Ausbildung, Lehre
(to) **arrest** [ə'rest] festnehmen, verhaften

B

(to) **bark** [bɑːk] bellen
bitch [bɪtʃ] *vulgär* Schlampe, Miststück
(to) **borrow** ['bɒrəʊ] leihen
(to) **breathe** [briːð] atmen
brick [brɪk] Ziegelstein, Backstein

C

carpet [kɑːpɪt] Teppich
(to) **carry** ['kæri] tragen
chapel ['tʃæpl] Kapelle
Christmas ['krɪsməs] Weihnachten
(to) **complain** [kəm'pleɪn] sich beklagen, sich beschweren
confused [kən'fjuːzd] verwirrt
(to) **continue** [kən'tɪnjuː] fortsetzen
(to) **cough** [kɒf] husten
criminal record ['krɪmɪnl 'rekɔːd] Vorstrafe
curly ['kɜːli] gelockt, lockig *(Haare)*

D

deaf [def] taub
(to) **dial** ['daɪəl] wählen *(Telefon)*
driving instructor ['draɪvɪŋ ɪnstrʌktə] Fahrlehrer(in)
driving licence ['draɪvɪŋ laɪsns] Führerschein
(to) **dye** [daɪ] färben

E

elbow ['elbəʊ] Ellbogen

expel [ɪk'spel]: (to) **be expelled from school** von der Schule verwiesen werden

F

frightened ['fraɪtnd] verängstigt
(to) **frown** [fraʊn] die Stirn runzeln
frozen ['frəʊzn] tiefgefroren
furious ['fjʊəriəs] wütend

G

glad [glæd]: (to) **be glad** sich freuen, glücklich sein
gravestone ['greɪvstəʊn] Grabstein
graveyard ['greɪvjɑːd] Friedhof
(to) **greet** [griːt] grüßen
(to) **grin** [grɪn] grinsen

H

hardly ['hɑːdli] kaum
hoodie ['hʊdi] Kapuzenpullover

I

inscription [ɪn'skrɪpʃn] Inschrift *(Grabstein)*

L

lead [liːd] (Hunde)leine
(to) **lie** [laɪ] lügen
(to) **limp** [lɪmp] hinken
loose [luːs]: (to) **let loose** von der Leine lassen *(Hund)*

M

memory ['meməri] Erinnerung
in loving memory in Gedenken an
motorbike ['məʊtəbaɪk] Motorrad
mug [mʌg] Becher

O

officer ['ɒfɪsə] Polizist
(to) **owe** sb. sth. [əʊ] jmd. etw. schulden

P

(to) **park** [pɑːk] parken
(to) **pat** [pæt] tätscheln *(Hund, Kopf, Schulter)*
pick-up ['pɪkʌp] *AE* Kleintransporter
playground ['pleɪgraʊnd] Spielplatz
pond [pɒnd] Teich
(to) **pour** [pɔː] gießen
(to) **pretend** [prɪ'tend] vortäuschen, so tun, als ob
prison ['prɪzn] Gefängnis
(to) **prove** [pruːv] beweisen
provisional licence [prə'vɪʒənl laɪsns] vorläufiger Führerschein
puppy ['pʌpi] Welpe, junger Hund

R

racing car ['reɪsɪŋ kɑː] Rennwagen
rat [ræt] Ratte

rather ['rɑːðə] lieber
realize ['riːlaɪz] erkennen, merken
(to) **recognize** ['rekəgnaɪz] erkennen
(to) **repair** [rɪ'peə] reparieren
rubble ['rʌbl] Trümmer, Schutt

S

sake [seɪk]: **for heaven's sake** *umg.* um Himmels willen
secret [siːkrɪt] Geheimnis
shape [ʃeɪp] Form, Gestalt
shortcut [ˌʃɔːt'kʌt] Abkürzung
(to) **shrug** [ʃrʌg] mit den Achseln zucken
(to) **sigh** [saɪ] seufzen
skip [skɪp] Container für Bauschutt
sled [sled] Schlitten
sleeve [sliːv] Ärmel
(to) **slip** [slɪp] rutschen, ausrutschen
(to) **sniff** [snɪf] schnüffeln
(to) **split up** with sb. [ˌsplɪt'ʌp] sich von jmd. trennen
spooky ['spuːki] gespenstisch, unheimlich
(to) **step** [step] treten, gehen
(to) **stumble** ['stʌmbl] stolpern
(to) **stutter** ['stʌtə] stottern
swing [swɪŋ] Schaukel
switch [swɪtʃ] Schalter
(to) **switch on** [ˌswɪtʃ'ɒn] anmachen
swot [swɒt] *umg.* Streber(in)

T

(to) **threaten** [θretn] drohen, androhen
tiny ['taɪni] winzig
torch [tɔːtʃ] *BE* Taschenlampe
(to) **toss** [tɒs] werfen
(to) **trust** [trʌst] vertrauen, trauen

W

wet [wet] nass
whether ['weðə] ob
(to) **wink** [wɪŋk] zwinkern
(to) **wish** [wɪʃ] wünschen
(to) **wrap** [ræp] einwickeln, einpacken

Check your understanding

Chapter 1 – 2

1 Who is Jason?
2 Who is Jane?
3 Where exactly does the party take place?
4 Why does Mortimer want to go to that party?
5 Describe Jason's flat. Do you like it?
6 When do they arrive at the party?

Chapter 3 – 4

1 Who are the party guests?
2 Why does Mortimer leave the party early?
3 Choose one person and describe him:
   a) Mortimer   b) Jason
4 Does Tessa like Jason's "practical joke" with the drink?
5 What would you do with the "wrong" jacket and the packet?

Chapter 5 – 6

1 Whose jacket is it?
2 Why does Mortimer think he can't go to the police?
3 Discuss with a partner: does Tessa know everything about Jason?
4 Why is Tessa in trouble at school?
5 Why does Mortimer want to see Tessa?

Chapter 7 – 8

1 What does Tessa do when she has problems?
2 Why does she argue with her boyfriend?
3 Who is with Jason when Mortimer runs into him on the playground?
4 Why is Mortimer afraid of Jason?
5 List pros and cons: should Mortimer give the drugs back?

Chapter 9 – 10

1 Why can't Mortimer find the jacket?
2 Why does he call Jane?
3 What is Jane watching on TV?
4 What is Jane's misunderstanding about?
5 When Mortimer switches on his TV he thinks of Jason's dog again. Why?

Chapter 11 – 12

1 Why is Mortimer still in bed at eight o'clock?
2 Why doesn't Mortimer want his mother's help?
3 What is the advice his mother gives him?
4 Do you think it is good advice?
5 Why doesn't Mortimer want to talk to Tessa about his problem?
6 Jason only laughs when Mortimer threatens to go to the police. Why is Jason not worried?
7 What does Jason want Mortimer to give him?

Chapter 13 – 14

1 Why did Tessa fall in love with Jason?
2 What does she think about her parents?
3 What lies does Jason tell her when she comes to see him?
4 What might Tessa think about after she leaves Jason's flat?
5 Why does Jason think that Tessa has become very boring?

Chapter 15 – 16

1 Where does Mortimer's father live?
2 Do you think Mortimer likes his brother?
3 Describe his brother and his father's wife.
4 Why does Mortimer tell his father that his computer may have a virus?
5 Do you think his father should give Mortimer his Christmas money when he asks for it?

Chapter 17 – 18

1 Why does Mortimer ask his father to take him to Tessa's house?
2 Why does he start stuttering when he's alone with her?
3 What does Mortimer tell her?
4 Why doesn't he want to confront Jason with his friend Paul?
5 Why doesn't he want Tessa with him in the graveyard?
6 What is their plan?
7 Why does Jason make fun of Mortimer?
8 What does Tessa realize when she hears that?

Chapter 19 – 20

1. Why is Mortimer afraid that Tessa could believe Jason more than him?
2. Why doesn't Chuck come back to Jason when he calls him?
3. Who comes to the graveyard to help Mortimer?
4. Why does Tessa come to the graveyard by bike?
5. What does Jason tell the police?
6. Why is his mother upset?
7. Why does Mortimer think it was his fault that Jason was so angry?
8. Do you think Mortimer and Tessa will go out with each other from now on?